THE GLAD GAME

by Phoebe Frances Brown

ISBN 978-0-573-00048-5

concordtheatricals.co.uk
concordtheatricals.com

FOR AMATEUR PRODUCTION ENQUIRIES

UNITED KINGDOM AND WORLD
EXCLUDING NORTH AMERICA
licensing@concordtheatricals.co.uk

020-7054-7298

Each title is subject to availability from Concord Theatricals, depending upon country of performance.

This work is published by Samuel French, an imprint of Concord Theatricals Ltd.

The Professional Rights in this play are controlled by Knight Hall Agency Ltd, Lower Ground Floor, 7 Mallow Street, London, EC1Y 8RQ.

office@knighthallagency.com

USE OF COPYRIGHTED MUSIC

A licence issued by Concord Theatricals to perform this play does not include permission to use the incidental music specified in this publication. In the United Kingdom: Where the place of performance is already licensed by the PERFORMING RIGHT SOCIETY (PRS) a return of the music used must be made to them. If the place of performance is not so licensed then application should be made to PRS for Music (www.prsformusic.com). A separate and additional licence from PHONOGRAPHIC PERFORMANCE LTD (www.ppluk.com) may be needed whenever commercial recordings are used. Outside the United Kingdom: Please contact the appropriate music licensing authority in your territory for the rights to any incidental music.

USE OF COPYRIGHTED THIRD-PARTY MATERIALS

Licensees are solely responsible for obtaining formal written permission from copyright owners to use copyrighted third-party materials (e.g., artworks, logos) in the performance of this play and are strongly cautioned to do so. If no such permission is obtained by the licensee, then the licensee must use only original materials that the licensee owns and controls. Licensees are solely responsible and liable for clearances of all third-party copyrighted materials, and shall indemnify the copyright owners of the play(s) and their licensing agent, Concord Theatricals Ltd., against any costs, expenses, losses and liabilities arising from the use of such copyrighted third-party materials by licensees.

IMPORTANT BILLING AND CREDIT REQUIREMENTS

If you have obtained performance rights to this title, please refer to your licensing agreement for important billing and credit requirements.

Small Island © 2019, Helen Edmundson
based on the novel by Andrea Levy
Published by Nick Hern Books
Used by permission

THE GLAD GAME was first performed at Nottingham Playhouse on 23 September 2021 and at Hampstead Theatre, London, on 9 February 2022. It was written and performed by Phoebe Frances Brown. The production was co-produced by Pippa Frith and Nottingham Playhouse, and supported by Arts Council England, Television Workshop, The Bush, and Hampstead Theatre. The performance was directed by Tessa Walker, with lighting design by Robbie Butler, sound design by Iain Armstrong, stage and production management by Maddy Wade. The assistant producer was Courtenay Johnson, and the charity partner was Brain Tumour Foundation. The voiceover cast included Waleed Akhtar, Aimee Berwick, Dominic Brown, Eamonn Brown, Gail Brown, Gemma Caseley-Kirk, Chloe Culpin, Stavros Demetraki, Haydn Gwynne, Sarah Hadland, CJ Johnson, Courtenay Johnson, Jake Kelsall, Lorna Laidlaw, Narisha Lawson, Manjeet Mann, Francesca Millican-Slater, Joe Powell, Sabrina Sandhu, Ben Welch and Alexis Zegerman.

DEDICATION

This play is dedicated to three very special men in Phoebe's life.

Dominic, her younger brother, who was a positive constant throughout her life and illness.

Jake, her boyfriend, who showed loyalty, commitment, understanding and love for her during their relationship.

Eamonn, her beloved dad, who we sadly lost sixteen months before Phoebe. He was her mentor, her sounding block, her inspiration and the driving force behind everything she did during her life.

She was so loved and is missed every day.

FOREWORDS

My fabulous daughter, Phoebe Frances Brown, aka Phoebe F***ing Brown, is the most inspirational, humorous, and highly talented person I've ever known (I'm biased, but it's true!).

She was a very independent and quietly determined little girl, and even as a toddler was totally self-driven and positive. She took control, organised her friends and cousins and led them into playing her games and performing plays, without them really knowing what they'd let themselves into. She was fun to be around, entertained everyone and enjoyed company. She was popular. A unique, wonderfully brave and determined human, who accepted her illness with hope and used it to live her life to the full.

This play is her realisation and acceptance of her future... her way of dealing with that knowledge. It's harsh, raw and not an easy read; it is, however, characteristically sidesplittingly funny at times. Life is cruel and unfair, but Phoebe's talent was to articulate her thoughts and feelings in her own unique way. *The Glad Game* is a guide, a self help manual and a lifeline for those left in a world without Phoebe F***ing Brown. It breaks my heart, but also fills it with so much love.

– Gail Brown

§

We're glad because...

We had the opportunity to work on this brilliant play with the amazing Phoebe Frances Brown. We saw the impact of *The Glad Game* on audiences, on Phoebe's friends and family and perhaps most importantly on Phoebe herself. She channeled so honestly into the play all her frustrations and fears but also all her light and her humour. *The Glad Game* is a brilliant piece of writing; heartfelt, honest and unique. Even though this piece is an autobiography, and an incredibly personal journey through an extraordinary experience, like all good stories it is universal and like all good plays it deserves to be brought to life again.

We hope that *The Glad Game* will be reimagined, shared with new audiences, its words read by other actors, directed by other directors, produced by other producers. It's what good plays need and it's what they deserve. This does not need to be your story to perform it. So please, make another production of it and make it your own, speak Phoebe's words, let it live on in new and exciting ways. Phoebe would absolutely love it.

– Tessa Walker and Pippa Frith
Director and Producer of *The Glad Game*

SPECIAL THANKS

There are far too many other people who need thanking for me to mention them individually. Their love, care and support for Phoebe, Dominic and me, has been extraordinary. Thank you, to all our wonderful family and friends.

– Gail Brown

§

Adam Penford, Stephanie Sirr and Tess Ellison and Nottingham Playhouse; Daniel Bailey and The Bush Theatre; Leicester Curve; Jake Kelsall; Narisha Lawson; Gemma Caseley-Kirk; Siobhan Cannon-Brownlie; Adam Kes Hipkin, Dan Hipkin and Oliver Bury at Tea Films; Nic Harvey; Television Workshop; Graham Elstone; Jenny Northam; Roxana Silbert; Sarah-Katy Davies; Lynette Dakin.

– Tessa Walker and Pippa Frith

PHOEBE. When I was dead little, I used to watch the Disney film *Pollyanna* at my Grandma's house. Recorded onto one of those blank video tapes. It's about a little girl called Pollyanna, she's an orphan and because she's an orphan she's moved in with her miserable Aunt who lives in a town full of miserable people, proper Debbie Downers the lot of them. I used to imagine I was like Pollyanna; no parents, plaits, paralysed. I was a strange child. But this little girl had enough courage and resilience to say, *"Yes...even in the saddest of times, there is always something to be glad about."* This is what she calls The Glad Game.

I'm an actor, aged twenty-eight, diagnosed with incurable brain cancer: this is my story.

§

Hi... I'm Phoebe...and I have a brain tumour, which is why I wasn't here yesterday... so... yeah just thought I should probably let everyone know now at the start 'cause if I look like I'm tired it's probably because I am.

Everyone's jaw drops.

I want to fall through the floor.

I'm glad because...
I'm glad because...
I'm glad because...

§

I'm actually fine by the way. I know what I just said sounds...not great but I really don't want you sitting there worrying about me, I'm all good. Honestly. I'm fine.

1

I will cry at some points and that's OK. I will have my script in hand because this is what a one woman show on chemo looks like. If you want to cry at some points too that's also OK. I will laugh at some points and I hope you will want to laugh too, I am giving you permission to laugh, please laugh? Basically, I don't want you to leave here today feeling miserable, that's the last thing I want; I'm here performing this show – I'm living the dream.

§

Poor Jake, he had no idea what he was letting himself in for when he swiped right for me. Six foot five, long hair, suitably quirky looking (he looks like a giant cartoon mouse – a sexy giant cartoon mouse). He's a filmmaker, I'm an actor.

We're both into the same Brazilian disco jazz fusion bongo funk.

We're both hideously clichéd and I love it.

It's just the second time I've stayed at his. I'm sat on the end of his bed, I stand up and I'm hit with a sharp pain, bright lights, I can literally see stars... I ring my dad:

(Dad voiceover:) "You should see a doctor about that."

My dad, Eamonn, enjoys every single cup of tea he has. He can have six in a day and he will savour every last drop. He's a huge Man City fan, he's maniacal about them so he's been there through the times when City were really shit to now, when they are really, really good – that's the extent of my football knowledge. He's such a big fan he used to have nightmares about Alex Ferguson. True story.

(Dad voiceover:) "You should see a doctor about that."

§

I go to Nottingham to film a sketch with my feminist, comedy sketch group: Major Labia. Me, Nish and Gem perform. Siobhan directs. We all write. We've all known each other for years. We all met at The Television Workshop, a drama group in Notts.

I can't put my finger on it, but I feel like something is really wrong with me.
I feel really panicky all the time. I just want to run away. There's something really wrong.
I feel like there's a gun to my head.

(Dad voiceover:) "You should see a doctor."

§

"I think I've had a migraine but I'm not really sure..."

(GP voiceover:) "Go and get an eye test."

§

Back to London, going about my everyday but every now and again I'm hit with these headaches. I wake up in a daze, stumble to the toilet, sometimes vomit. Like I'm starting every day with a hangover, groggy and shitty and also getting anxious about feeling groggy and shitty...

November 5th. Bonfire night.
Wake up, feel awful. Force myself out of bed, neck pains now which are new.

When I ring my mum to tell her she tells me to come home to Nottingham.

Now.

§

My mum, Gail, is a primary school music teacher and a bloody good one at that. She runs several choirs, recorder groups and directs the year six production in the summer term each year. She's pretty much out every night doing something or meeting friends. I don't know this yet but my mum will become a Super Mum. She'll tell me to believe in miracles, and I will. Mum is an inspiration.

§

At St Pancras. Feel really weird. Panicky. Not right. Ring my parents in tears. Beg them to pick me up from the station. The train is overcrowded, stuck in a carriage with not just one but two crying babies. I feel every screech and yelp rattle through my body. My head is fucking killing. Dad meets me off the platform. Ring the doctor's when we're in the car. Rush hour and the traffic is so bad. It's dark, get out of the car, it's bonfire night. My head is fucking killing. Rockets scream and bang, bang, BANG. What's that? Surely not another screaming baby in the waiting room? 100 points for Gryffindor! In between his cries, the squealing catherine wheels and the fireworks, I have to rest my head in my hands. Scared it's about to cave in.

§

(GP voiceover:) "You should have had an eye test. I'm going to prescribe some low dosage antidepressants, Amitriptyline. Have some paracetamol and go to bed."

I get home and vomit.
I'm in bed for three days.
I have an eye test. There's nothing.

§

Stress.
Stress and anxiety.
Living in London trying to be an actor is enough to give anyone a nervous breakdown, never mind a little migraine.

So the most logical thing is to move back to Nottingham with my mum and dad. The ultimate fail. I'm embarrassed and ashamed and so disappointed in myself. There's no way out.

"I feel like there's a gun to my head..."

§

In London. Say goodbye to Jake. We've been seeing each other quite a lot these last few weeks. It feels nice but I'm going so...

I'll see you when I see you then.

§

My brother Dom is helping me move. Been a difficult morning. My room is the basement flat so after I haul a bag up the stairs I have to stop and have a little lie down before he goes down to bring up the rest.

(Dom voice note.)

"Yo! Pretty mad I just got a voicemail of you actually, I was literally just going to send you one. Just been for a swim. Did eighty lengths, off the bounce, sorry about that, sixty all off the bounce which is like a kilometre of straight swimming which I was buzzing with... On the way home in the car that Chaka Khan song came on *(Sings.*)* so I had a proper Phoebe Phoebe moment which was cool... I'm having Bournville, which is like cocoa, on a piece of toast. It's bloody lovely!

I was genuinely going to ring you after the Chaka Khan moment in the car *(Sings.*)* but yeah... I'll love you and leave you."

---

* A licence to produce *THE GLAD GAME* does not include a performance license for any third-party or copyrighted music. Licensees should create an original composition or use music in the public domain. For further information, please see the Music Use Note on page iii.

Dom drives me back to Nottingham.

Like my dad, my brother loves sport. He's obsessed. Particularly with cricket. And he's particularly good at it. Cricket is quite like acting. We've had many discussions about this. Dom always says to me, "you know when you go into an audition, it's like going up to the crease. You're letting them know, you're Phoebe Fucking Brown. Do you know what I mean?" And you know what, I do know what he means.

"I'm Phoebe Fucking Brown, I'm Phoebe Fucking Brown, I'm Phoebe Fucking Brown."

§

Back to the doctors.

(GP voiceover:) "What are you worried about?"

"That I'm not getting better –"

(GP voiceover:) "No – what are you worried about?"

"Well, that I don't seem to be improving and it's starting to affect my vision –"

(GP voiceover:) "Are you worried it's a brain tumour?"

I feel like there's a gun to my head.

(GP voiceover:) "I'm going to send you for an MRI scan."

§

I do a Major Labia rehearsal with Siobhan, Gem and Nish. I'm seeing double.

I go to Siobhan's thirtieth birthday on Saturday. Siobhan is completely obsessed with Bruce Springsteen. She's gifted a life size cardboard cutout of 'The Boss', which she's grinding up against.

I'm wearing dark sunglasses.

Inside.

At night.

If someone is stood in front of a light, I can't see them.
I'm basically blind now.
I sit outside on the curb with Nish. Nish is also a nurse.
She sits with me as I wait for my cab. I tell her I think
there's something really wrong. I know there is. I'm
scared.

§

On the way to the MRI. Can't look out of the window.
Head down the whole way because it's making me feel
dizzy.

Scan over. Get home. Get into bed. The landline rings
almost immediately.

(Dad voiceover:) "They've said you need to go to
Queen's Med now –"

Silence.

All the way there.

Arrivals.

We wait. And wait.

Told it's bad enough to have to stay the night but
no-one explains to us what's going on;

(Doctor voiceover:) "From what we know, there's
something but we're not allowed to disclose what it is…"

Moved to a private cubicle. I have some morphine.
Lights off. I can't see properly.
Wait.
Nap.
Wait. For another six hours.
And as though we're in some black, black, blacker
than black comedy, a pneumatic drill starts pounding
away at the wall.

(Dad voiceover:) "Would you be able to get my daughter some ear plugs please?"

(Nurse voiceover:) "Yeah, yeah one sec."

...

(Nurse voiceover:) "I don't have any ear plugs but I can get you an eye patch?"

(Dad voiceover:) "Sorry – what is going on? Look, my daughter has been waiting."

(Nurse voiceover:) "I'm really sorry, sir."

Finally, we're moved up to the next floor.

More waiting.

I am getting frustrated. I am getting really angry. My head is fucking killing.

Seven hours later.

(Doctor voiceover:) "I'm just going to cut to the chase. We haven't actually seen the scans but from what has been described over the phone you have a large mass on the left side of the brain. We have to operate. We won't be able to take all of it out. I do think we can do this."

§

"Have you heard of Charly Clive, the star of Channel 4's hit show *Pure*..."

Every person I speak to says:

"Have you heard of Charly Clive, the star of Channel 4's hit show *Pure*, she's got a brain tumour too and she made a show called *Britney* and isn't she just an all-round amazing and inspiring person..."

Bitch, stole my idea.

This is supposed to be my thing.

My awful story turned good.

So I actually did an audition for *Pure* with Charly Clive, she'd already been cast as the lead. I was reading for the part of her only real 'friend' in London. She had a brain tumour and, at the time, unbeknownst to me, I had a brain tumour.

Her face is everywhere.

Her face is FUCKING EVERYWHERE.

FUCK OFF

FUCK OFF

FUCK OFF.

Then I watch *Pure* and she's absolutely brilliant.

I watch it midway through my radiotherapy. I don't want to, I really don't want to because I'm scared. I'm scared because if she's shit, what will that mean? I'm scared that if she's good, what would that mean? I'm scared that if she's really, really good would that just make me want to die? But she's absolutely brilliant. She makes me think that if she can do this, I can do this.

Because you have to be really optimistic to want to be an actor and you have to be really bloody optimistic to want to be an actor when you have a brain tumour.

So:

Charly Clive, star of Channel 4's hit show *Pure*. You gave me some fucking hope, hope in probably the bleakest time of my life. You helped me heal.

Thank you Charly Clive.

§

A floaty day. Due to the drugs. A weirdly calm day.

After the whirlwind of the day before it feels good just to be able to sit.

Mum, Dad and Dom are with me. It feels like Christmas because we play games.

The Major Labia girls arrive, it's emotional. I crack funnies but super sad funnies.

Siobhan gives me an eye mask and ear plugs.

Gem gives me some stones for healing.

Nish gives me some crisps.

It gets closer to my next MRI scan and I begin to feel panicky.

Ink pumps through my veins to highlight the tumour.

Salt tastes as though it's in my mouth.

It's louder, more uncomfortable.

I lie still for the longest time.

Back in my room, the nurse gives me a massive hug. It's such a big, lovely hug. And it goes on for a while.

I really need to speak to someone. Anyone. Please.

Betty, the chaplain, arrives. I tell her everything. All of my frustrations and anger. My relief at finally knowing what's wrong with me.

(Betty voiceover:) "Firstly, you must believe in your doctors. You must trust them. It is so important."

I'd never considered it from that angle before.

(Betty voiceover:) "Secondly, there are two kinds of people who come into hospital. Those who come in sick and those who come in and get sick. You will get through this. It's going to be hard but trust me, you're fit and healthy and you will get through it."

(Betty voiceover:) "It's all a lot right now but trust me, you will be fine."

I will be fine.

I'm glad because...
I'm glad because...
I'm glad because... A few months previous. Appointment notification: Audition for *Small Island* at the National Theatre. Part: Queenie, the lead. Director: Rufus Norris, the Artistic Director. Stage: Olivier. The biggest bloody stage in the theatre! I'm Phoebe Fucking Brown. Do it. It's one of the best auditions I've ever done. Get fab feedback.

(Casting director voiceover:) "She did very well. Please thank her very much. She's very talented."

Wait.

(Agent voiceover:) "It's gone to someone else."

Forget about it.

§

My consultant,

(Consultant voiceover:) "It is a massive brain tumour. It's been there for a very long time. This has been resting on your drive and motivation, which is why you've probably been finding it hard to get up in the morning. Yours is an extremely rare case. Brain tumours are graded so if it's a grade 1 that's usually just kids, grade 2 is slow-growing and is benign but can still be life-threatening depending on where it's growing and how big it gets and grades 3 and 4 are higher grades of cancer. Your GP will be shocked to find out you have such a large brain tumour. You're going to be the talk of the town."

Paul Byrne, brain surgeon, or God, as I like to call him, assures me:

(Paul Byrne voiceover:) "I won't have done my job successfully if you come out harmed in any way..."

So if I can't speak, or I'm paralysed or I die – that won't be good...

He tells me I may have to do radiotherapy and chemotherapy. He tells me it's mainly grade 2 but on the scans it looks like there are signs of it possibly transforming into grade 3.

I'm not going to think about that.

§

Now you may have forgotten about Jake. Sexy cartoon mouse guy. Well we've been texting this whole time. I told him about my MRI, he replied saying "to check there aren't aliens eating at your cerebral cortex?" Have my first phone call with him this evening confirming it is aliens eating at my cerebral cortex. He laughs. A sad laugh.

We speak for two hours. A mixture of things; sad things. Hilarious things. I tell him the whole story.

(Jake voiceover:) "I need to come and see you."

This is so much. It's almost too much for me... it's been so lovely but we've only known each other for two months so I'd absolutely understand if you just want to leave it here...

He says he's never felt like this before.

He tells me it doesn't matter if I'm going to get sick and that if we can get through this, we can get through anything.

We say goodbye. It's late. I look around my hospital room, the sink, the bed, the empty chair and think... oh my god! I've actually got a boyfriend!

Next day.
The Major Labia girls and Dom come. They come bearing gifts.
Dom brings a pack of cards.
Siobhan and Gem bring a little flower in a reindeer pot.
Nish brings me some crisps.

A joyful time if a little melancholic.
A day of waiting. And waiting.
Waiting for my meds.
Waiting for my final eye examination.
Waiting for my consent form. The consent form is grim. Like fucking grim.

(Nurse voiceover:) "So do you suffer from seizures at the minute?"

"Umm no?"

(Nurse voiceover:) "OK because that might happen but we can give you meds for that."

"Right OK."

It's Friday. My operation is booked for next Wednesday. Five days' time. I'm laden with leaflets and instructions for meds. When I'm finally discharged, I burst into tears.

I'm glad because...
I'm glad because...
I'm glad because... I get my hair cut by Shaun.

(Shaun voiceover:) "It's just not fair is it? I mean when you think there's paedophiles and mass murderers and the like walking the street and then there's you with your – it's not fair."

Emma comes. Emma is my super posh, super lovely university friend. Emma's big claim to fame is that she used to live in the house from the film *Notting Hill*, the one with the blue door. True story. She flirts with Shaun, telling him all about it and he loves it.

My mum is just there, smiling.

Jake's coming to Nottingham to see me. He's going to meet my parents for the very first time, we've only being going out officially for three days. He tells me he needs some Dutch courage so he is a bit pissed when he arrives. He gets out of the cab with his arms flailing about like Mr Tickle. *(Pretends to be him.)* "Whaay hello." Dad shakes his hand. Mum gives him a hug.

The drink works because he charms them good and proper.

Jake hates the idea of being romantic. It actually repulses him. Yet staying with me, whilst barely knowing me, is the most romantic gesture in the world.
He'll see me at my worst, and he will see me at my best and he will see me at all the bits in between.
He loves me.
He makes me a playlist of jazz tunes he thinks I'll like. In hospital and for the next few months these songs will feel like they are running through my veins. They'll keep me sane. I'll cry to songs on that playlist. I'll smile. When I'm not strong enough to stand, I'll get really good at chair dancing and sway and shimmy and dance my little heart out...

§

The night before my op and I can't sleep.

Nish sends me a voice note.

(Nish voice note.)

"Well, well, well if it isn't Phoebe Frances Brown hey? Good evening! How are you? This is literally a quick one as I know you're going to try and get an early night because you've got brain surgery tomorrow do you know what I mean? Going to try and rest up. But this is like a... I want to say 'all the best' for tomorrow or 'good luck' or 'I've got my fingers crossed type of thing' but I just don't think that's the right tone if I'm really honest with you it's like, it's not an audition... But 'have faith'. I've got so much faith in the doctors, in the NHS, in the process, in YOU and your body and, do you know what I mean...? There's no words to be like 'don't get scared' or 'be brave, be strong'. It's like, look it is what it is but you are absolutely bossing it like a pro. You know what I mean. Like honestly. You've overcome so much. This is no different. It's like a small little hurdle. You go for a little brain op in the morning and bish, bash, bosh by the afternoon, you know what I mean, you're laughing. No. On a serious note. Honestly. I just have so much faith that everything is going to go all as planned and you're probably going to wake up like, wow. It's done. Yes I'll be in touch obviously as soon as you wake up! Everyone wants to be there like 'Hi Phoebe! How are you?' Erm. But I'm going to just text your mum to let me know maybe when you're awake, maybe when it's okay to have visitors because the next three days also you probably don't want to see anyone but yes I love you lots and lots and lots and lots and I guess yeah, I'll speak to you tomorrow you massive fucking rat. No I'm joking. I love you so much. Bye bye."

Paul Byrne, neurosurgeon.

(Paul Byrne voiceover:) "I have done this procedure many times before."

"I'm not worried. See you in a bit."

Eyes close.

Eyes open.

I'm back in the bay I had been before, I have no idea if I'd been moved from the area or not, it's twenty past two.

I'll see later in the mirror my scar looks like a fleshy plait across where my fringe would be. My hair is crispy from the blood. My front teeth have a gap in them that wasn't there before.

My head feels physically lighter as if a brick's been removed from my brain, my neck stops hurting immediately.

I ring Jake from my hospital bed on the ward. I can only text people love heart emojis because my brain isn't working properly. It takes me forever to make him understand I just want to hear him speak and to tell me about his day and I'll be here listening.

The first few nights are terrible.

I hear my skull slowly moving and readjusting like the earth's tectonic plates.

I hear a whirring in my ears, the blood pumping round my body.

I hear a ticking inside my head all the time, so loud at night, like my head is an empty exam hall and the school clock ticking terrifyingly loud.

Directly after surgery. I'm well confused and well emotional. I hear a nurse speak. She's reading my notes to another nurse and I don't know whether she thinks I'm unconscious or not…

(Nurse voiceover:) "Phoebe Brown, 9th November 1992, craniotomy and debulking for a left frontal primary brain tumour, grade 3…"

My family arrive. They look so pleased to see me alive and well but all I can think is grade 3, grade 3, grade 3…

I'm glad because...
I'm glad because...
I'm glad because... A few days later. My agent Joe.

(Agent voiceover:) "You've had an offer from The National for *Small Island*. It's for a smaller role, Franny and ensemble, and you'll be the understudy for Queenie..."

    (Beat.)

I GOT A JOB AT THE NATIONAL FUCKING THEATRE.
ON THE OLIVIER STAGE AND IT'S DIRECTED BY RUFUS FUCKING NORRIS.
A job at the National.
The National.
I got the job.
I got the job.
I got it.

You couldn't write this shit.

(Surgeon voiceover:) "So, your tumour is an Astrocytoma. It is a grade 3, which means it's a higher grade of cancer and it's aggressive. This means I won't ever be able to stop it but just slow it down and manage it. We would recommend you do thirty rounds of radiotherapy and then a year's worth of chemo. You will have to come back regularly for scans..."

"OK. Can I do this job that starts on Feb 18th?"

(Surgeon voiceover:) "Yes, and you should. It might be tight with the radiotherapy but let's see if we can fast track that. You have to carry on –"

I ring my agent Joe.
I have to do the job. I need to.

I also need to let friends know.

I message Gemma. Gemma is my funny, little creature friend from Gedling. I can just imagine her huddled over a cauldron casting love spells in her sexy, witchy, pixie voice.

"WARNING SAD MESSAGE BELOW.

Morning btw Laughing with tears emoji but I feel like I need to tell you it is grade 3 which means it's malignant. They won't ever be able to get rid of it but just slow it down. I've youth on my side and I'm fit and healthy so it should be manageable, but I felt like you needed to know the full disclosure"

"So that's good?????"
"But sad"

This is genuinely what she sounds like. True story.

"Yeah good but sad"

"But good still the same"
"It can be like your companion"
"Of life"
"But we need to make sure it shuts its gob"
"Don't be sad beautiful"

"Phew"

Hand clapping emojis from Gem.
"I'm so happy it's not aggressive"

     (Beat.)

"No it is aggressive"

     (Beat.)

"That's what malignant means"

"Omg I have never read something so wrong"
"Oh noooooo"
"I'm such an idiot I'm so sorry ahahaha"
"Oh boo so but the radiotherapy will shoot it right"
"So it won't hurt you"

"Yeah it'll slow it... I'll be fine"

Slow it down.

I go into town and feel numb. Get home and feel anxious.
Slow it down. Keep going over it. Slow. It. Down. Slow. It. Down. Not stop it. Not remove it.
Not destroy it, just slow it down.
There's a bomb in my head and it's tick, tick, ticking all the time and one day it's going to explode and kill me.
I think I'm having a panic attack.

(Macmillan Support voiceover:) "Hello Macmillan Cancer Support what can I help you with today?"

I just had my diagnosis today.

(Macmillan Support voiceover:) "Right OK and how are you feeling about it?"

Not good. I'm twenty-six and I have a grade 3 Astrocytoma.

(Macmillan Support voiceover:) "OK. That must've been a lot to take in."

Yes and it's all just cracked off in the last few weeks.

(Macmillan Support voiceover:) "Do you feel like you're careering down a ski slope and you can't stop?"

Yes.

Dom gets home.

We hold each other and cry.

"You're who I talk to, Pheeb. I don't speak to Mum or Dad, I speak to you. This happens to other people; this doesn't happen to you."

It's proper sad.

"I know. Hopefully I'll still be about but I also might not be about forever so it's probably a good idea to start speaking to Mum and Dad a bit more than you do."

Mum and Dad come upstairs and we all crawl into my bed and hold each other and cry.

It's proper, proper sad.

I'm glad because...

I'm glad because...

I'm glad because... Chloe. Chloe is a friend from University, also from Nottingham, I met her on the first day of our Drama course, we discovered we had loads of friends in common, thought everyone else on our course was a weirdo and have been friends ever since.

So, Chloe suggests a country walk. She suggests Padley Gorge, it's in the Peak District, it's basically Sheffield. We drive. It's nice. It's raining. It's stunning. Beautiful in fact. It's woodland and you can see the rushing water down in the gorge below.

We start the walk down this huge, rocky mountain.

I start to notice a lot of hazards; big stones, which are slippy; steep decline, which is slippy; mud, which is slippy and a sheer drop down into the gorge itself. Slippy. It starts to dawn on me, how on earth are we going to get back up?

We get to the bottom and have a little rest at one of the weirdest cafés I've ever been to; you order your food, get a raffle ticket and sit down and then a guy on a mic shouts out your number. It was quite a small café, why he needed a mic, I don't know.

At the bottom of what was quite a treacherous walk, we start to climb all the way back up. I don't want to get Chloe stressed but I can feel my legs wobbling as I heave them up this steep incline. I start to feel tired, it's getting darker, I think if I have to stop, we've got no phone signal, it's getting darker, how will she get in touch with anyone, what if I need an air ambulance, it's getting darker, wetter and colder, I can see Chloe getting slightly panicked but also trying not to get me panicked which is in turn making me panic more. This walk is pretty difficult for the fittest of people, never mind someone who's TWO WEEKS OUT OF MAJOR BRAIN SURGERY!

Finally. We scramble back to the car. Cranking the wheel at the side of my seat to recline it as flat as I can. Lie back. Corpse pose. Chloe definitely thinks she's killed me.

§

Christmas.

I've been quite nervous about Christmas Day. I cry over breakfast, but I think it's because Radio 2 was playing some emotionally manipulative bullshit. But I'm actually fine. It's a standard Christmas Day – not the best but not the worst. No, I retract that, it's absolutely the worst Christmas Day but it just isn't as bad as I thought it would be.

Jake drives over. We do a quiz and Jake and I absolutely bitch-slap my dad and brother at the movies round. We are that proper smug couple who everyone else hates but it doesn't matter what anyone else thinks because we're in love so fuck you.

After Boxing Day he drives me to Coventry to meet his parents. I can't drive anymore, not since the brain surgery. I was a terrible driver anyway. I once drove into three parked cars so I think it's safe to say the roads are a lot safer now. On the way I get a call:

(Jo voiceover:) "Hi Phoebe, it's Jo from the Speech and Language department at Nottingham University Hospital. You've been referred to us, would you like to book yourself in for an appointment?"

Yeah, no errrm ermmmm no errrrm language... no yes no... alright my language, so erm no, errm no errrrm I don't think I need it.

(Jo voiceover:) "I'm going to book you in for the 30th Jan."

Later that night Jake says to me:

"It's when you get nervous. It's with people you're not as comfortable with so with me you're fine but you've got to try and push yourself because you're not as snappy or as quick witted as you once were –"

My hands rush up to cover my face. I try not to show I'm crying.

"No, no I don't mean that it's just –"

"No you're right. I know I'm not and I hate it. Like tonight, for example, I wanted to talk. I wanted to talk so badly to your parents, but I just couldn't. I know I'm not myself and I'm not on my best form and that's what's really upsetting because I used to be confident and could take situations like this, like 'meeting the parents' in my stride –"

"– And you will again. You've just got to do some rewiring that's all. It's been three weeks since you've had major brain surgery."

§

I'm Phoebe Fucking Brown; this shouldn't be happening to me.

I've worked so hard on being confident and the thought of having to build myself up again – well, I'm just going to have to do it again aren't I? Because I have always backed myself. From day one. Even when I wasn't confident, I backed myself. Even when I was a scared little eleven-year-old, who wouldn't volunteer herself to go in the middle of the circle for my Television Workshop audition and when my two best friends from primary school got recalls and I didn't, I backed myself. I went to a state school by the way and I know we shouldn't go on about it but fuck it, I did! I then went to a Russell Group Red Brick University and GOT A FIRST and then didn't go to drama school BECAUSE I COULDN'T AFFORD TO and then worked my arse off for three long years, doing temp jobs as well as acting jobs – one of my temp jobs was working for a waste removal company, as thrilling as it sounds – before I finally got signed by Joe the Lord and Saviour Powell at one of the best agencies in the country. I've been to New York with a show, I've performed at the Donmar Warehouse and at The National Theatre in London and I feel like I'm only just getting started. It's because I am, only just getting started. I'm at the start of my career and to have this emotional, invisible, hideous turd dumped on me now – well it takes millennial quarter-life crisis to a whole new level. It's a sick fucking joke. It's beautifully cruel; to lurk in the shadows of my brain for so many years and to suddenly make an appearance now, and to not only make an appearance, this tumour by the way, is on the left side of my brain, and it's located right where my speech and language and my memory is. Nice one. Good one. I know, what does Phoebe love more than anything in the world, the thing she has sacrificed holidays for, travelling for, would have dropped anything for: acting, where it's quite useful to be able speak and remember lines. You don't have to do much to be an actor. Except those two very basic things. Oh, you're a cunt. A fucking cunt. I hate you so much. I am going to show you, yes you, that this bitch, and yes I'm reclaiming the word bitch right here, right now, does not go down without a fight. This bitch does not take prisoners. This bad ass motherfucking bitch is not going anywhere. Just yet. I've got too much shit to do first.

Next morning, feeling pumped, ready for the day and ready to talk to Jake's mum. Come on now, Pheeb, you've got this, we all believe in you, show her who's boss:

"I've got a money plant."

(Jake's mum voiceover:) "Oh have you? Yeah this plant I think I've had it for about, well it must be about, it must be about twenty-five years now."

"Wow."

(Jake's mum voiceover:) "Yeah I know!"

"That's amazing."

(Jake's mum voiceover:) "So where's your money plant now? Do you take it with you when you go to London?"

"Well it's a funny story actually, it's really funny errrm it is really funny so I left it at ermmm ermmm errrm a flat, the flat... So I left it at the flat of my ermmm errrm my friend's...and it was called, it had a name...erm, ermmmm, wait, what was it called? Its name? Sorry this isn't a funny story at all, HA, what was it called?"

Maybe it was living in London. Yep London, the big city, bright lights and fuckloads of smog. Because I was fine in September and perhaps when it was "possibly transforming into grade 3" it all started kicking off around then. Maybe that's bullshit because I had a massive panic attack at Edinburgh Waverley Station at the end of the Fringe. Maybe it was all around the time I had to decide between doing a run with Major Labia or doing a TV show with Dawn French (I didn't do the TV show). Maybe it was before that, when I was in a very stressful relationship during a really exciting transition to London, actually London and actually at the Donmar Warehouse, where my then boyfriend decided to break up with me basically on press night. Maybe it was before that, when I was working on *Life According to Saki*, another Edinburgh Fringe show and had another stressful unrequited 'Fringe Fling'. Maybe it was the year before that when I was broken up with by the boy who'd already dumped me once before. Maybe it was final year of Uni – I mean, need I say any more? Maybe it was second year of Uni, probably one of the worst years of my life living with my ex-boyfriend and, at the time, the love of my life, and being able to hear if he had or hadn't come home... Maybe it was the year before that, first year when I would cry every time I was drunk because I wished I'd gone to drama school. Maybe it was final year of sixth form when I didn't know whether to go to Uni and do a drama degree or take a year out and then try for drama school, oh no wait I can't do that because that's when the coalition happened so £9000 the fees would be if I were to take a year out. You know what, I blame the government. I do. Because of the government, this Tory government, who we will be governed by for the next five fucking forever, rent prices in London are extortionate, mortgage? don't even know what that is but then that wasn't all this government's fault was it I mean Blair was basically Thatcher in disguise and actually it's Thatcher's fault because come on, it's all her fault isn't it? I mean she sold off the council houses, the energy companies, she basically is the definition of what neoliberalism is. I BLAME NEOLIBERALISM. Because of you, the government, Trump, Brexit, 9/11, Iraq, the Arab Spring, Palestine, Israel, ISIS, McDonald's, Tesco, Amazon, Google, Facebook, Instagram, because of you –

you've ruined the best years of my life. Or maybe, these have been the best years of my life and they will continue to be the best years of my life and cancer is fucking cruel and random and I can't think about what might happen to me. About what is potentially going to happen to me. I can't even go there. I can't. I won't do it. It's too frightening. And fuck being frightened.

Monty was the name of my plant – by the way.

§

New Year's Eve.
Dom thinks it would be a good idea for me to have a party.
A big day. Get up early, do lots of tidying, do lots of cooking.
All of my friends come; friends from school, friends from University, friends from Television Workshop.
We have sparklers for the countdown.
It's a proper, lovely evening.
1.30 a.m., bit late for me, Sister Nancy, "Bam Bam" plays.
I stir the vegan stew.
I'm having a laugh with Nish.
I start stammering "duh duh duh" Nish thinks I'm being silly but quickly realises that this isn't a joke.

I fall back
I feel like I can't breathe
Everything goes black.
I genuinely think, *this is it*.

Then I come back round, it must've only been less than a minute.
Paramedics arrive.
Party's over people.

Back in A&E.
CT scan. Long wait for the results. Again.

(Doctor voiceover:) "It's quite normal for this to happen post brain surgery: When you've been poking about in there there's bound to be a little hiccup every now and again. There's some scar tissue and residual tumour on the part of the brain that controls your speech and language which is why you found yourself stammering and a shock wave went across your brain. Seizures can be caused by tiredness so I'm going to treat this as an isolated incident. Now were you drinking?"

Nope.

(Doctor voiceover:) "OK. Good."

Jake's been to his own New Year's Eve party in London. I ring him from the cubicle as he's walking home, it's about 9 a.m. He says

(Jake voiceover:) "I think you might be the scariest person I know."

§

"Hi... I'm Phoebe...and I have a brain tumour, which is why I wasn't here yesterday... I was having my last session of radiotherapy in Nottingham and I will be doing chemo as well so... yeah just thought I should probably let everyone know now at the start 'cause if I look like I'm tired it's probably because I am."

Everyone's jaw drops.

I want to fall through the floor.

CJ gets us all to hold hands.

(CJ voiceover:) "We're all here and we're all sending positive vibes to you."

The women of colour in the company tell me they'll bring headscarves for me tomorrow, that they'll help me.

The magic of theatre at work.

Each day I get stronger and stronger. Mum and Dad notice an almost overnight transformation. I'm happy again. Actually happy. I remember who I am and it feels so good.

In week two, Aisling who is playing Queenie is down with chickenpox *so*, a little sooner than expected, I'm called up from the bench. Me. With a brain tumour.

This time we're not in the rehearsal room we're on the friggin Olivier and it's time, my time.

On the stage, I look out at the sparsely populated auditorium, house lights up, and I feel like I've arrived.
I perform as Queenie.
Talk to the empty seats.
Connect.
I feel like me again.
I do it for me.
Me.
And I'm home at last.

Week three, I'm fully joining in; getting stronger physically, mentally and emotionally. I feel brighter.

Wednesday I get up, get ready, have my breakfast. I have a slight headache, get off the train early at Waterloo to get some paracetamol. I quickly walk to the theatre, a walk I hadn't attempted yet but I feel alright so fuck it.

Get there, feel tired. I just need a lie down before I go into rehearsal.

Go back when I feel ready. We're doing movement. A flick of a newspaper on the one count of eight and then change direction of walking.

I can't do the move. My right hand feels weird. I've been told to refer to these as auras, my brain's way of warning me I'm about to have a seizure but the meds

I'm on now mean I never lose consciousness and have a fit. I then feel myself stammering but only very quietly.

I walk out of the rehearsal room.
Get myself into my dressing room and onto the bed.

I wait for it to pass and it does.

I break down.

My aura, I caught it.

You cocky twat.
You cocky, cocky twat.
You cocky, stupid, fucking twat.

I get taken home in a cab. I go upstairs to bed.
Jake says:

(Jake voiceover:) "What are you like, eh?"

Next day my agent Joe comes round:

(Agent voiceover:) "You've been relieved of your understudy duties."

I love Queenie. Learning her lines was the one thing that kept me going over Christmas, New Year, radiotherapy. It's more than a part to me.

(Agent voiceover:) "They really want to make it work, Phoebe. When you're well enough, you can do Franny. Who wants to be the fucking understudy anyway?"

"Yeah... When do you think they'll let me back?"

(Agent voiceover:) "Don't know yet."

Phone goes. It's Chloe:

(Chloe voiceover:) "How do you feel about a camping trip with Rosie and Vicky? I have a family tent Laughing with tears emoji"

I mean... I'm just not on camping tbh

(Chloe voiceover:) "Fair Laughing with tears emoji"

Told I can sit in on rehearsals: "to observe but not participate."

This waiting. Constantly waiting, waiting to get back on stage, waiting to finish chemo, waiting to finish radiotherapy, waiting for surgery, waiting for my final eye examination, waiting for my consent form, waiting and waiting and waiting and waiting for what? I don't have time to wait. It pisses me off when I have to wait for Chloe because she's always late; this is my time; my precious time and I don't have lots of it. I'm well aware, every birthday, Christmas, New Year might be my last.

I watch my teammates from the sidelines and think... will I ever be able to do this again? Be in a company of actors again? Will I ever be in a play again? Will I ever work again? It's the Press Night. I'm still waiting. In the audience. Observing. Watching the understudy play Franny, hear her say my five lines. The show is beautiful. Everyone involved does such a fantastic job. It breaks my heart to not be up there with them, taking my bow as the audience give a standing ovation. I stand with tears rolling down my face. This isn't even funny anymore, I want to scream. I want to dig my heels in. I want to grab onto the chairs in the auditorium. I REFUSE TO LEAVE THIS THEATRE! I REFUSE TO LEAVE THIS THEATRE! LET ME GO BACK ON STAGE!

I'm glad because...
I'm glad because...
I'm glad because...

Cancer Rehab Gym Class

I've never been very good at exercise. Not flexible enough for yoga, not fast enough for running, not strong enough for squats. At school, I always came last in every single race on sports day. It was humiliating. I've been scarred ever since.

(Lou voiceover:) "Hello everyone! I'm Lou and I'm here today to get you all moving!"

So when I receive a letter inviting me to the Cancer Rehab Gym Class, I am dreading it.

(Lou voiceover:) "Can we go round the circle, introduce ourselves and say what we want to achieve by the end of the eight weeks."

Looking round. I'm the youngest, by far.

Vanya, great name, age seventy-four, says he wants to be able to dance the salsa like he used to.

Betty, mid 80s, in her south London smoker's gravel, says she wants "to be able to get to the bottom of my road without getting out of breath."

What is my life...?

I'm Phoebe and I don't really know...

(Lou voiceover:) "I'll just put down 'improve general fitness'. Is that alright?"

Yep.

Lou introduces us to some pretty intense gym equipment. Proper treadmill, proper leg press, proper bike machine thing. There's proper floor work, like planks, crunches, press ups.

(Lou voiceover:) "Let's get moving!"

Vanya is pulling up one kilogram dumbbells to the beat of the music.

Betty's walking on one of the two treadmills, the other one's free. She's looking at me like, what you waiting for? What am I waiting for? What am I fucking waiting for? I should be making my way to the National now, catching the 68 to Waterloo. But instead I'm here. Next to Nance. In the Cancer Centre. I reluctantly get on and start walking. Fall in sync with the music. Marching at the same time... it's very slow for me. A dilemma presents itself. I'm walking next to the woman who's basically got one lung... I don't know what to do, so I tentatively start jogging... not so bad... might try a bit faster? And faster? OMG. I'm running! I'M RUNNING. Feel like the fastest in the room. I am the fastest in the room! I'm never the fastest in the room!!

(Lou voiceover:) "WELL DONE PHOEBE!!"

This is the best day of my life!

(Lou voiceover:) "Three, two, one and change!"

Crunches.

(Lou voiceover:) "AMAZING PHOEBE. Three, two, one and change!"

Press ups.

(Lou voiceover:) "PHOEBE, GOOD JOB! Change!"

Cross trainer.

(Lou voiceover:) "WOAH, PHOEBE SLOW DOWN!!"

I'm getting hot in the face. Not just from the exercise but from the constant praise. I'm loving it.

It's bang on twelve. Right about now, I'd probably be having lunch in the canteen just before the matinee...

(Lou voiceover:) "To finish the class we're gonna do a Wii session of 'Just Dance'. Would anyone like to lead?"

ME!

Please.

It's time. My time.

(Upbeat music plays.*)

Woo! Betty's right behind me, copying my every move. Laughing. And coughing. C'mon now! Out of the corner of my eye, I can see some snake hips, slithering their way towards me... it's Vanya... the drawstring on his joggers looks like it's about to take someone's eye out. Wahey!! Lou's boogying away at the back of the class.

Rehab Gym Class is a riot!

Yes, I am the most flexible, the fastest and the strongest in a class of three, where two are pensioners, but I've got to get my kicks from somewhere.

So Lou, where do I sign up for next week?

Woo!
And then. After all of the waiting and the confusion. Joe gives me the go ahead from the National.

(Agent voiceover:) "They say, if you feel well enough, they would love for you to resume as Franny."

Back in rehearsals.

Everyone's watching.

Small Island is about the Windrush Generation and it's set in London and Jamaica during the Second World War. Franny and Queenie are work colleagues at a rest centre in London. This is my first go at the scene. I'm Phoebe Fucking Brown!

---

* A licence to produce *THE GLAD GAME* does not include a performance license for any third-party or copyrighted recordings. Licensees should create their own.

Franny starts the scene so in my best cockney accent I say "'ere!" to Queenie, "'ave some PC3s" – PC3s were documents to help people who'd had their homes bombed.

Aisling replies, "I'm that tired, I don't know whether I'm coming or going."

Oh, to hear another actor say those lines back to me instead of my mum. Sorry Mum.

To some, five lines might not sound like a lot but it's a great little exchange; there's so much subtext to play with. Franny's basically asking Queenie if she can bonk someone in her house next weekend. Or at least, that's the way I'm playing it. "Ah well, worth a try."

Sit down. A glow of pride washes over. Not just from me but from all the members of the cast and production team. They're all proud of me. I'm back.

§

My first show.

My parents and my brother and all of Major Labia are here in the audience.

Siobhan brings me some flowers.
Gem brings me some incense.
Nish brings me some crisps.

Jake's with me backstage. I can't tell if these nerves I'm feeling are normal or not. What even is normal now?

I've got my wig, costume, mic on; now it's time to wait.

(Stage manager voiceover:) "Phoebe Frances Brown to stage. Phoebe Frances Brown to stage please."

I walk onstage, "...Oh, I've got favour to ask – could you put a flight crew up for a couple of nights? End of next week?" I can feel the PC3s shaking as I hold them. Beattie, a member of the cast grabs my hands, it's OK – we've got you. "Ah well, worth a try."

I've done it. I've actually done it. I've done it! I want to go out there again and do it again and again. Please. I want to live out there. It's easier. It's simpler. I can forget for a few moments, I can forget everything and it feels amazing.

Phone goes. It's Chloe. Fancy going zorbing?

§

I say my five lines.

With every show I feel all of my anxiety, depression, worry just lessens, bit by bit, day by day.

I do all the shows in the last week, I didn't feel confident enough to do them until then.

There's this feeling of shame and embarrassment that comes with a cancer diagnosis. We've built a society where we feel we have to apologise and feel guilty about being sick.

I'm not apologising. Yes, I'm tired and I'm going to be tired for the rest of my life – get over it.

§

A Pollyanna, according to The Oxford Dictionary, is an excessively cheerful or optimistic person. I am neither of these things and if anything I think if I knew a Pollyanna, I'd find them really annoying. Some things that happen in life are terrible and I'm not gonna say this is easy because it's fucking not and I wish this wasn't my story, but it is. So I will carry on and if I do lose the ability to speak and remember lines, I'll just have to make a beautiful improvised mime show.

I'm glad because...I've got such an amazingly supportive family.

I'm glad because...I ended up with a boyfriend, what the actual fuck?!

I'm glad because...I have the best friends I could have ever wished for.

I'm glad because...I live in a country where I get all my health care for free.

I'm glad because...I've proved to myself I do have the courage and resilience to do anything.

I'm glad because...I'm Phoebe Fucking Brown. I'm alive and I'm here.

Milton Keynes UK
Ingram Content Group UK Ltd.
UKHW021841310324
440266UK00018B/754